W9-AXT-452

© Franklin Watts 1988

Designed and produced by
Aladdin Books and David West
Children's Book Design
70 Old Compton Street
London W1V 5PA

First published in the
United States in 1988 by
Franklin Watts
387 Park Avenue South
New York, NY 10016

ISBN 0 531 10573 3

Library of Congress Catalog
Card Number: 88-50491

Printed in Belgium

This book is not intended as a substitute for the medical advice of physicians. The prospective mother should consult a physician in matters relating to childbirth or other aspects of her health.

This book is dedicated to Vance, Katti, and Daniel, with thanks to those who helped their parents bring them into the world safely and in good health.

CONTENTS

TEEN · GUIDE · TO

CHILDBIRTH

FERN G. BROWN

Franklin Watts

New York · London · Toronto · Sydney

Chapter One:
Getting Ready to Birth Your Baby

Having a baby is a natural part of life. But to aid in a safe, comfortable delivery, expectant moms – and dads, too – need to know what is going to happen during the birth process and to prepare themselves for this important event.

You've carried your baby almost full term. In the past nine months, there have been many changes in your body. Now it's time to get ready for your baby's birth. Of course you want a safe delivery and a healthy child.

You are looking forward to becoming a mother. When your baby moves inside you, it is a good feeling. But like many pregnant women, you have other feelings too. One of the most common is fear. It's the fear of not knowing what to expect.

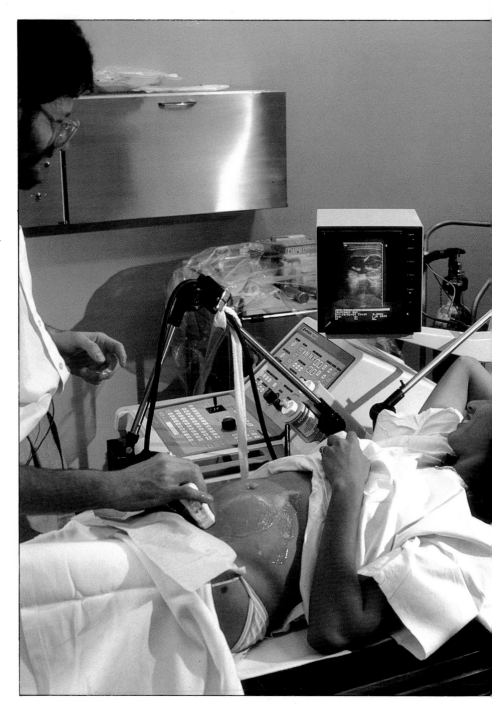

Tests are sometimes carried out to check the health of the unborn baby.

Having a baby is no mystery. Birth is a healthy, normal process. Knowing what's going to happen can make it much easier. You'll be able to handle it better.

There is more than one way of getting ready to have a child. And there is more than one way to deal with **labor**. Methods differ with each place or person who helps with birth. Read books, take classes, and talk with your doctor or **midwife**. Pick the program of care that is best for you.

Childbirth classes are a good idea. There may still be time for you to take a few. You'll learn about the choices you have; for example, places to birth your baby, and positions during labor.

Some questions may bother you. How will you know when your baby is about to be born? What are **labor pains**? Does having a baby hurt? The **birth educator** will answer your questions. Friendly classmates can help too.

To find out about classes, ask your doctor or midwife. You can also telephone the maternity division of a local hospital.

Visit the place where you've chosen to deliver your baby. Talk to women who have had babies there. Be sure that the person who assists you is well trained.

Knowing what to expect will take much of the fear out of childbirth. You'll deliver your baby with flying colors.

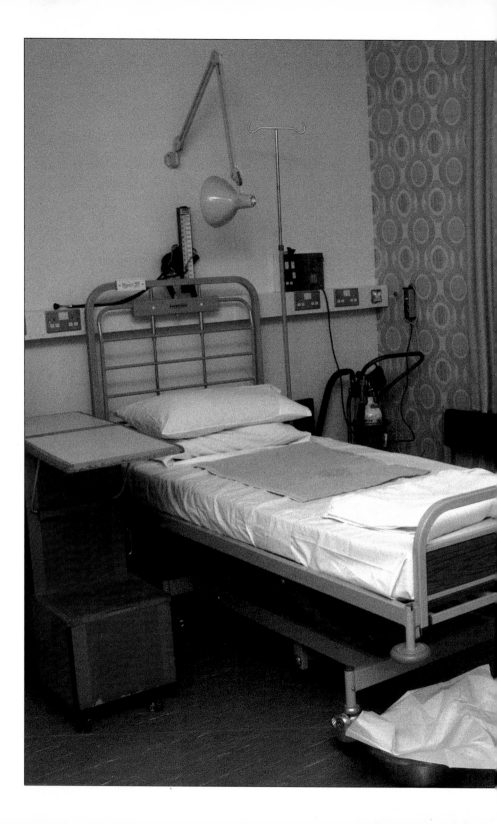

Chapter Two:
Place of Birth

Although some babies are born at home or in a birthing center, most are delivered in a hospital by an obstetrician. Hospitals are not only governed by strict health rules, but also have up-to-date emergency equipment should it be needed.

Where will you deliver your baby? You have several choices.

Hospital Birth

"We like the hospital best because it has a maternity wing with separate labor, delivery, and recovery rooms," Joyce said. "I feel safe and comfortable there."

"Bet you can't find more up-to-date equipment anywhere," Paul said. "Besides, our hospital also has a **high-risk unit**. If Joyce has a problem during labor or delivery, she'll have expert care."

A hospital birth is thought to be safe and low-risk by most people. One doctor said, "Nobody can be sure of what will happen during the last minutes of a delivery. If there's an emergency, it's best to be in a hospital. The time it takes to get there could mean the difference between life and death."

There are couples, though, who think a hospital delivery room is not the best place to deliver a baby. They say hospitals have too many rules. They want to birth their babies in a more natural way, and have more say in how they're born.

Because mothers are asking for more choices, many hospitals are now giving them what they want. For example, in some hospitals the mother may use a birthing chair to deliver sitting up, instead of lying down. New fathers may be allowed to stay overnight. And sometimes babies can room-in with their mothers.

If you decide on a hospital birth, ask for what you want. You may not get what you ask for. But don't be afraid to ask. It all depends on the doctor and the hospital.

The Birthing Center

An **alternate birthing center**, or **ABC**, can be a homelike **birthing room** in the maternity wing of a hospital. It can be connected to a hospital but separate from the maternity wing. Or it may be in a building with no connection to any hospital. All ABCs have one thing in common. Labor, delivery, and recovery take place in one room.

Gina and Ed chose an ABC on hospital grounds. "Our room looks just

The positions in which a woman can give birth are shown here: (a-b) lying on her back, (c) squatting, (d) sitting in a birthing chair. In the sitting and squatting positions, the pull of gravity helps the woman as she pushes the baby out during delivery.

like a bedroom in our apartment," Ed said. "We've even got a stereo."

"It's the best of both worlds," said Gina. "We're having our baby in a nice, homey place. And if I should need them, emergency equipment and trained people are nearby."

Gina is happy that at her birth center both Ed and her mother can be with her during the entire labor and delivery. She thinks they will be a big help. Afterward, Gina plans to have the baby room-in. She doesn't want the infant put in a nursery.

"I think our ABC is the best place for bonding," Gina said. **Bonding** is a special feeling of closeness and love between newborns and their parents. It takes place right after the baby's birth and lasts through time.

To attend her baby's birth, Gina chose a **certified nurse-midwife** (CNM) who had given her prenatal care. A CNM is a registered nurse who has worked with pregnant women for at least a year. After finishing a graduate midwifery program at school, the CNM must pass a written exam and get a license from the state in which he or she intends to work.

If you decide on an ABC, visit several and pick the one that suits you. Some freestanding ABCs have no hospital connections. It may be difficult to get emergency care in them. Check to see that the ABC you choose has a backup hospital.

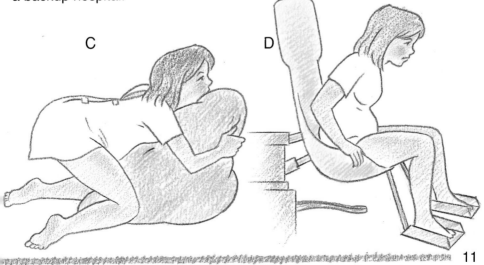

C D

Having Your Baby at Home

Joanne and Craig wanted their baby's birth to be as natural as possible. So they took classes and prepared to have their baby at home. They learned what to expect during labor and delivery.

Most doctors are not only against home births, they refuse to have anything to do with them. They say that there are too many risks, that the mother and child are exposed to unnecessary danger. The people attending the birth may not be well trained. The birthplace may not be clean enough – or may not have the right equipment. Also, in a possible emergency, a hospital may be too far away.

"We know the risks in home birth," Joanne said. "But we don't expect complications."

Many home births are attended by lay midwives. They usually get on-the-job training with experienced midwives. Or they work under the direction of doctors. In some states home births with lay midwives are illegal. In others, lay midwives must have a license or permit to practice. The laws are different in different states. Joanne chose a lay midwife and a doctor to attend her.

And if there is a problem?

"We live close to a hospital," Craig said. "We can get there within minutes."

Your baby will probably be born without any trouble. But be aware of the risks if you decide to give birth at home. You must have good prenatal care, and well-trained, experienced people to attend you. And most important, there should be a backup hospital nearby. You will have to get there quickly if a problem comes up that can't be handled at home.

In short, a home delivery is great if nothing bad happens. If something bad happens, it could be a disaster. Why take the risk? Although Joanne found a doctor she liked to attend her, there aren't many experienced obstetricians who will attend home births. Home birthing is a choice, but there is much more risk connected with it than the other choices we've mentioned.

How Do You Make Choices?

Long before you are ready to deliver, get pamphlets and books from your doctor. Talk to new mothers. Ask them to tell you about their birth experience and what they found helpful.

Hospital nurses in **obstetrical (OB)** units are usually happy to help. They can give you the phone numbers of birth educators.

A childbirth class is a good place for information. If you aren't in a class, you can call a childbirth teacher and ask questions anyway.

Discuss your options with your partner. Decide what type of birth suits you best. Then pick the birthing place and choose people to attend you who share your ideas.

This may seem like a lot of work. But it takes time to shop for things like clothes and records too, doesn't it? Your baby is surely worth the effort.

Cost and Insurance

Hospital costs vary. Even with insurance, many policies don't pay 100 percent of the hospital maternity costs.

If you are considering a birth center, check to see whether your insurance will cover the birth and any problems that may come up. A birth center may save you money over a hospital birth. That's because you and your baby could go home within twenty-four hours.

Nurse-midwife fees are usually covered by insurance. But few policies cover lay midwives and home births.

More Things to Think About

Before your delivery discuss with your doctor or midwife how last-minute problems will be handled. Ask questions such as, "How will decisions be made?" "What if I need a cesarean?" and "What type of **anesthetic** will be used?"

Balance your hopes for the type of delivery you want with cost, convenience, and safety for you and the baby. You may have to make a trade-off. For instance, the doctor you want may not practice at the ABC you like best. Or your birthing plan may hit a snag because of a problem. Have a second plan ready. Don't think you've failed if your second plan is put to use.

Be Prepared

For the hospital or birthing center: Preregister. Keep your doctor's or midwife's telephone number handy. Pack a bag with your personal things at least three weeks ahead of your due date. Pack another bag with baby clothes and a blanket. You may want to include a loaded camera and film, a small radio, and food and drink for your **labor coach**. Don't forget a safe

Mother's bag
Toiletries, nighty, slippers, clean clothes.

Baby's bag
Baby clothes, diapers, blanket.

car seat for the baby.

Arrange beforehand for someone to drive you to the birthing place. Have a cab number and money on hand in case of an emergency.

For a home birth: Get equipment ready. Have clean clothes and bedding for you and the baby. Be sure there is enough food in the house. Have a camera loaded with film. Arrange for a backup hospital in case of an emergency. Line up a **pediatrician** to examine the baby within twenty-four hours of birth.

Wherever you choose to deliver your baby, be prepared. Then you'll have a good, safe birth!

Chapter Three:
Prepared Childbirth

One of the best ways to get ready for labor and delivery is to attend a childbirth class. Although there are several types to choose from, all have a common goal – the well-being of mother and baby during the birthing process.

Joyce was in her third **trimester** of pregnancy (twenty-eight to forty weeks). She was getting nervous about labor and delivery. Her doctor thought perhaps a **prepared childbirth** class would help her.

Does Prepared Childbirth Help?

Joyce asked her friend Betsy if childbirth classes had helped during her delivery.

"You bet!" Betsy said. "I was nervous as a cat until I went to class. My instructor taught me how to handle labor and delivery. I was in charge, so my delivery was a piece of cake. I only needed a little medicine at the last moment," she said, proudly.

Joyce was sold on prepared childbirth. She looked in the phone book under Childbirth Education to find a class near her home. But she was confused. Should she call Lamaze, Bradley, or Read? And what about the other methods that Joyce had never heard of? How do you choose a childbirth class? she wondered.

A good way to choose a childbirth class is to learn all you can about the various methods. Then pick the one that suits you.

Natural Childbirth

In the 1930s an English obstetrician named Grantly Dick-Read attended a woman who felt no pain during birth. It amazed him. He'd thought that pain was always a part of birth. Afterwards, he came up with the idea that no mother-to-be had to feel pain. He said the reason most of them did was that they'd heard too many horror stories about labor. They thought birth was painful, and it made them afraid. That fear, he said, brought on muscle tension. And it was muscle tension that caused them real pain.

Dick-Read said that if women learned to relax, and trusted their doctors, they wouldn't need medicine for pain. He developed a method called Childbirth Without Fear, or Natural Childbirth. It is the basis of all our childbirth education today.

Expectant mothers were told by Dick-Read to train for childbirth like an athlete trains for a race. He said they should get enough sleep, eat a balanced diet, and exercise daily.

Although he believed in natural birth without medicine, Dick-Read didn't let a patient suffer. He gave anesthetics when there was a need.

Lamaze Method

Fernand Lamaze, a French obstetrician, combined ideas from a Russian method to prevent pain with Dick-Read's natural childbirth. Then he added several ideas of his own. Lamaze developed a new way of breathing to control the pain of the contractions and the tensing of the muscles. And he taught support from a coach — usually the baby's father. In addition, he explained to women in detail how their bodies worked. Each class included breathing, relaxation, and delivery exercises. Mothers-to-be were told to look forward to the moment of birth with joy, not fear.

The Bradley Method

Dr. Robert Bradley was the first American obstetrician to form a method of childbirth without medicine. He said that if human mothers let nature take over, they would give birth as naturally as farm animals did.

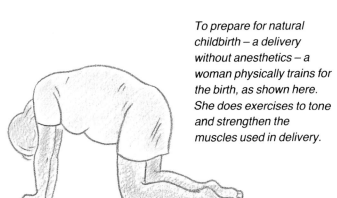

To prepare for natural childbirth – a delivery without anesthetics – a woman physically trains for the birth, as shown here. She does exercises to tone and strengthen the muscles used in delivery. She practices breathing exercises. This is a rhythmic, evenly spaced breathing in and out. This helps her to cope with the pains of labor and to keep the muscles relaxed. Tensing the body increases labor pain.

Most Bradley classes are taught by couples who have taken instruction and birthed a baby by that method. They teach a special way to breathe and relax during labor.

Bradley wanted natural birth to take place in a hospital. So he worked to change hospital rules. He was the first American doctor to allow fathers into the delivery room as labor coaches.

Mothers attended by Bradley breast-fed their infants on the delivery table. It wasn't unusual to see a woman who had just given birth walk into the recovery room with her baby in her arms. The babies roomed-in with their mothers. Bradley disliked hospital nurseries. He called them "kid concentration camps."

The Leboyer Method

Read, Lamaze, and Bradley worked with mothers. French obstetrician Frederick Leboyer worried about the babies. He said that babies felt pain and shock when they were born under bright delivery room lights. In his book, *Birth without Violence*, he wrote that babies should be born in dim lighting with music playing. As soon as possible, they should be gently bathed in warm water. Mothers and attendants must speak in whispers.

Many women have delivered their babies by Leboyer's method. They say their infants are especially content. Mothers who have given birth in a traditional delivery room say there's no proof that Leboyer's method has any long-term benefits. Their babies are content and happy too.

Other Methods

Now there are many new prepared childbirth methods. Most of them have taken ideas from Dick-Read, Lamaze, or Bradley, and have added ideas of their own. But all the methods have certain things in common. They teach pregnant women about their bodies. They do relaxation and breathing exercises. And they have a support person at the birth to help the mother.

You may choose one of these methods to birth your baby. Or you can take a part of each and combine it into your birth plan.

Joyce's Choice

Joyce picked two methods she liked. Then she called the instructors. She asked questions such as, "How big are your classes?" "How much will they cost?" "Can my support person come too?"

She chose a low-cost YMCA Lamaze class. It was limited to eight couples. She went to the class with Paul, the baby's father. Besides discussing labor and delivery, the class talked about the risks and benefits of using hospital equipment such as fetal monitors. They also talked about the different types of medicines available. Within a few weeks, Joyce felt more relaxed and confident about her baby's birth.

Paul was taught to be Joyce's labor coach. "I like helping Joyce," he said. "Being her labor coach makes me part of the birth of our baby."

Does Lamaze really work? It worked for Joyce's friend Betsy. "When I felt pain," Betsy said, "I'd look at the teddy bear I'd brought. I'd picture my baby playing with it. Then I'd remember to breathe right and relax. I did have to ask for medicine at the end, but I was in control most of the time."

Is Natural Childbirth Good for You?

Natural childbirth is a good way to have a baby. If you're not having problems, why take medicine? On the other hand, you may plan to deliver your baby naturally but find you can't go through with it. Don't think you've failed. You and your coach are only human, and you're doing your best. Just remember, no matter which method you plan to use to birth your baby, it's important to be relaxed, comfortable, and in control.

Chapter Four:
Early Signs of Labor

As you approach your due date, you will want to start watching for signs that labor will soon begin. Unusual bursts of energy, swollen legs and feet, an occasional tightening of the abdomen – these are all important signs.

As Joyce's due date drew near, her baby wasn't kicking as much as it had been. That was because it was almost full-grown and there was less room to move around.

Suddenly Joyce began cleaning the kitchen cabinets. This sudden burst of energy is to be expected. "Paul thought I went bananas," Joyce said. "But Mom called it the nesting instinct. She told us she cleaned the basement thoroughly the week before I was born."

Joyce and Paul talked over their birth plan. They went to see films on birth at the hospital. Although she felt big and "klutzy," Joyce practiced her Lamaze exercises every day. She wanted to be in good shape when she went into labor.

What Is Labor?

During pregnancy, the baby grows and develops inside the mother's body. All the changes her body goes through end in labor. During labor many things work together to get the baby out of the mother's **uterus** (womb) safely. You may think labor and delivery are two separate parts of giving birth. Actually, they are both part of the same series of actions and changes. Delivery is the end result.

What Happens When You're in Labor?

The upper part of the uterus is made of smooth muscle. It opens up and spreads out as your baby grows inside you. During the last weeks of pregnancy the upper part of the uterus stops spreading. It begins movements to pull together. These movements are called muscle contractions.

At the same time the lower part of the uterus begins to stretch. It prepares the tube-shaped **cervix** to **efface** (shorten) and **dilate** (widen) so

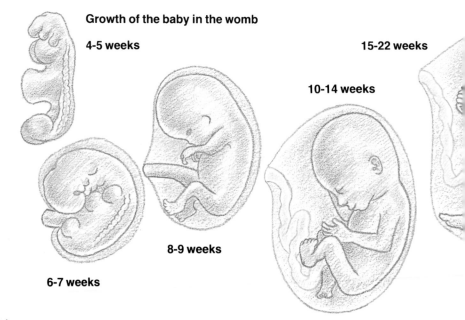

Growth of the baby in the womb

4-5 weeks

15-22 weeks

10-14 weeks

8-9 weeks

6-7 weeks

the baby can come out.

You might say that labor consists of many muscular contractions that push the baby downward. The contractions thin the bottom of the uterus and the cervix. They help to pull the cervix back over the baby. The birth canal is getting ready. And the baby is eventually pushed down the birth canal and out into the world.

Think of labor as something like putting on a turtleneck sweater. Every contraction moves the baby's head down the birth canal. The canal gets shorter and thinner. When you put your head through a turtleneck, the neck of the sweater, like the birth canal, gets shorter and thinner too.

What Is Prelabor?

Your uterus has been contracting since the beginning of your second trimester. You probably haven't noticed the contractions. That's because they've been weak and far apart.

About four weeks before birth, the uterus contracts more and more often.

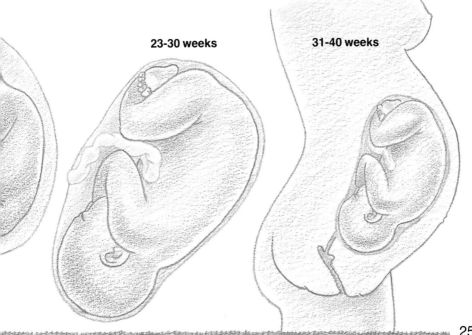

23-30 weeks   **31-40 weeks**

You may feel a tightening of the abdomen that lasts for only a minute or two. It may be uncomfortable – sort of like menstrual cramps.

In the last two weeks of pregnancy these contractions can happen every ten or twenty minutes. They are known as Braxton Hicks contractions after Dr. John Braxton Hicks, who first described them. The contractions get the uterus ready for actual labor. They also help the circulation of the mother's blood to the **placenta**.

When Braxton Hicks contractions get closer together and last longer, they are called false labor. These contractions do some work. But they stop before completing the job. And they don't affect the cervical opening.

There isn't any test to tell false from real labor. Some doctors feel there is no difference between the two. They say all of the contractions help to prepare the cervix and uterus for delivery. So, they are all a part of real labor.

When Joyce felt the Braxton Hicks contractions, she said, "I watched my belly tense in the middle and then spread around to the sides. But I didn't do anything about it." She smiled. "I just kept busy cleaning cabinets."

Joyce's last pelvic exams were uncomfortable. During the exams, she did relaxation and slow-breathing exercises. They helped a lot. She spotted a little afterwards. The doctor said it was nothing to worry about.

Signs that Birth Is Near in First Babies

One way to tell that birth is near is when you feel the baby lightening or dropping. It means that it is gradually dropping down into the **pelvis**. For first-time mothers, it usually happens two or three weeks before delivery.

How will you know when your baby has dropped? Your stomach will be farther out and lower down. You'll breathe easier, and feel more comfortable after eating. But you may have to make many trips to the bathroom to empty your bladder, because of pressure on your pelvis.

When Joyce's baby dropped, her legs and feet swelled. She could barely walk. But she knew that labor was that much closer.

Another sign that labor is near is something called **bloody show**. Right after the baby is conceived until just before delivery, a **mucous plug** seals off the mother's cervix. It keeps the uterus germ-free. Later on, when the cervix dilates and stretches, the opening gets very wide. The plug slips out. When this happens, the mother will see a brownish or pinkish blood-tinged mucus coming out. This bloody show might be seen hours or days before labor begins. But it's often so small an amount that many women don't even notice it.

In the uterus the baby is surrounded by **amniotic fluid** held in by two membranes. They are called the **amnion** and the **chorion**. These membranes line the inside of the uterus. Once the mucous plug is gone,

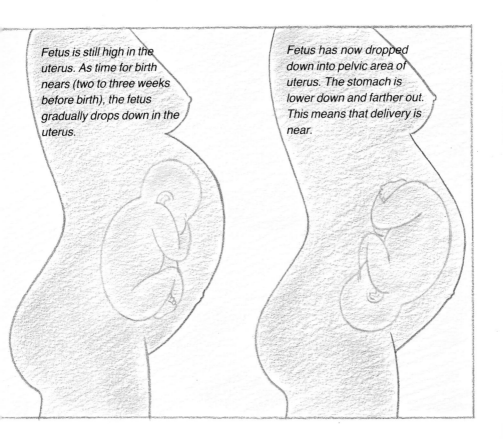

Fetus is still high in the uterus. As time for birth nears (two to three weeks before birth), the fetus gradually drops down in the uterus.

Fetus has now dropped down into pelvic area of uterus. The stomach is lower down and farther out. This means that delivery is near.

the membranes show. They fill the center of the dilating cervix.

In between the membranes and the baby's head there is a liquid called the **bag of waters**. When the membranes break, this clear liquid flows from the **vagina**. It often comes out in a gush. But sometimes the baby's head acts as a kind of stopper. Then the fluid drips out a little at a time.

Your bag of waters may not break before labor begins. But be prepared in case it does. It's a good idea to protect your mattress with plastic as your due date comes closer.

When Joyce went into her third trimester, her Lamaze instructor laughingly told her to carry a jar of pickles. "If you're out when your bag of waters breaks," she said, "you won't be embarrassed. Just smash the jar of pickles on the spot and nobody will know what really happened."

Once the membranes have burst there is an open pathway to the baby. It is important to call your doctor or midwife immediately.

If you're delivering the baby at a birth center, they may tell you to come in at once.

Forcing Labor

Sometimes a doctor will try to start, or bring on, labor. But if it's done, there are certain risks to the baby. So most doctors won't do it without good reason. They must decide whether continuing the pregnancy is a bigger risk to the baby than bringing on labor.

A doctor may decide to force labor because the mother is past forty-two weeks of pregnancy. Or perhaps because her bag of waters broke too soon and labor did not follow. Or because the mother has a disease that creates a medical reason for forcing labor.

One way to bring on labor is for the doctor to break the bag of waters during a pelvic exam. Another is to give the mother medicine, such as pitocin. Sometimes both ways are used together.

How Do You Know When You're in Labor?

Joyce's due date had come and gone. At the last pelvic exam her doctor had told her that her cervix was one or two centimeters dilated, and at least partially effaced. She had seen the bloody show the day before. But her bag of waters had not broken. She was feeling contractions, but they weren't coming too often. Was it false labor, or the real thing? Should she call the doctor, Joyce wondered?

Before you call the doctor ask yourself some questions. How long have you felt the contractions? How often do they come? Is the time between them getting shorter? Do they feel stronger now than when they started?

If you still aren't sure whether or not it's false labor, change your position. Stand up if you are sitting. If you are lying down, get up and walk. Or take a warm bath (if your membranes haven't broken). If its Braxton Hicks the contractions will often stop.

But if the contractions don't stop, labor has probably begun. How soon you should call your doctor or midwife depends on how far you are from the hospital or birth center, or if you're delivering at home, how far your attendants have to come.

If you haven't far to go, don't rush. It can be nerve-wracking to get to the hospital or birth center too soon. But when you live pretty far away, it's better to be early than late.

If you are about to check in and the contractions stop, you may want to walk around for a while. Walking during labor is good for you. Or perhaps you'd rather read or watch TV in a lounge. The longer you avoid the labor room, the shorter labor will seem.

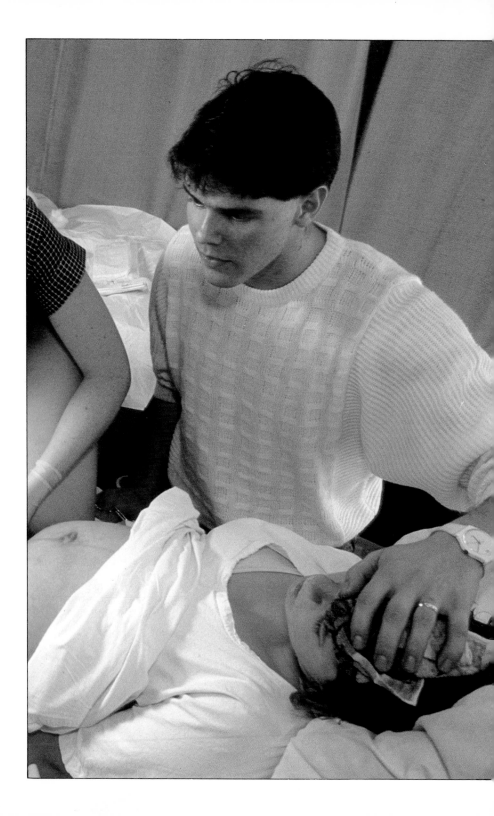

Chapter Five:
The Four Stages of Labor

During the first stage of labor, the contractions begin. As the contractions come more often, you will need to keep your breathing even, controlled, and relaxed.

We're not quite sure what brings labor on. And there is no way to tell exactly when it will begin. When Joyce's due date came and went, she said, "I hated to answer the phone. All I ever heard was, 'Hi, you still there?' It really bugged me."

Joyce was making dinner when suddenly her bag of waters broke. She was prepared for her baby's birth. But when labor actually began, it surprised her. She stood and watched as the clear liquid gushed out onto the kitchen floor. Then laughing and crying, Joyce reached for the mop. She said aloud as if she'd first realized it, "Hey, we're having a baby."

It's important to note the color of the liquid of your bag of waters. If instead of being clear, it's a shade of green, tell your doctor. You and the baby will be watched carefully during labor to make sure that the baby doesn't have a problem.

After her bag of waters broke, Joyce's doctor told her to time her contractions. She was to come to the hospital when they were five minutes apart, and lasting sixty seconds. Now that the bag of waters was gone, the doctor explained, germs could reach the baby. Since Joyce had carried full-term, it would be best if her baby was born within twenty-four hours.

FIRST STAGE OF LABOR

Early Phase

There are four stages of labor. The first stage is divided into three parts. The first part is called the Early Phase.

A nurse monitors a patient's blood pressure.

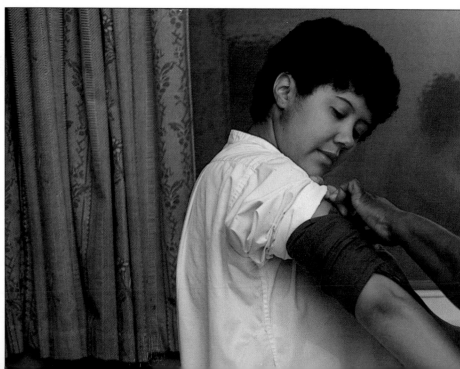

For Joyce, labor began gently. If it weren't for the breaking of the bag of waters she might not have noticed the change in the contractions. She used a watch with a second hand to time the contractions. During the first hour, they came almost every ten minutes and they lasted for about twenty to thirty seconds. They didn't stop when she lay down or took a shower.

Like Joyce, you may go through the early phase of labor without much pain. During this stage your cervix will shorten and widen to three centimeters (1 1/4 in). The contractions may feel like menstrual cramps. It might take up to ten hours to get to four centimeters. Be patient and trust your body. Things go faster after that.

Joyce called Paul and her parents. She drank some sugar water, for energy, and recorded every contraction.

When Paul came home, Joyce didn't stop talking. She was happy one minute and scared the next. She paced up and back. He didn't stop her. He

knew that walking was good for her.

The contractions were eight or nine minutes apart. Paul tried to keep Joyce calm and relaxed. He suggested a game of Scrabble, but she couldn't concentrate. So he put on the TV.

It took two more hours, but at last the contractions were five minutes apart. Paul called the doctor. Then he and Joyce drove to the hospital. Since they had visited there many times, they knew what to do.

Joyce had preregistered. So she went right to the labor room. Paul parked. Then he joined Joyce with her labor bag.

Each hospital and birth center has a different way of doing things. The doctor or midwife leaves a set of orders for every patient. Or the hospital or birth center has a general policy that everyone follows.

At Joyce's hospital she was asked to put on a hospital gown. A nurse asked about her medical history, allergies, whether the bag of waters had broken, and what she had eaten during the last four hours. She took Joyce's temperature, blood pressure, and felt her pulse.

Next Joyce was told to lie in bed for a vaginal exam. This exam was done to see how far her cervix had effaced and dilated. The position of the baby was checked.

There are two terms that describe the position of the baby. They are **presentation** and **station.**

Presentation means the part of the baby that is coming down through the pelvis first. This can actually be felt during the exam. The majority of babies come down headfirst.

Station refers to where the baby's head is in relation to the ischial spines. The ischial spines are the lowest of the three major bones that make up the pelvis. They are used as a boundary line. Zero station is level with the ischial spines. Anything above it is called a minus station. Anything below is a plus station. The baby's head will be at the plus-four station when it reaches the place where it's ready for delivery.

Vaginal exams will continue throughout labor. During them, the mother should breathe slowly and try not to tense up.

Labor causes the body to lose water and to use a lot of energy. So sometimes the doctor sets up a line to put fluids and sugar back into the veins. The line is called an IV. Medicine can be given quickly this way too.

Prepping

Prepping is the term used for the pubic shave and enema.

In the past, enemas to clean the bowel were thought necessary for all mothers. But now they are not given unless ordered by the hospital or doctor.

To avoid germs, shaving of pubic hair was usually ordered for most mothers. But today the thinking is that shaving itself may cause germs. Some doctors order a "mini-prep" instead. The hair around the **labia** is cut with a scissors. With this the mother doesn't have the itching that happens when shaved hair grows back. But often doctors and midwives don't order any shaving or cutting for their patients. And it is very seldom done at birth centers.

Fetal Monitors

During labor, many doctors and midwives follow the baby's heartbeat with an electronic external **fetal monitor**. And sometimes an internal monitor is used too.

The baby's heartbeat gives a general idea of its health. Changes in the heart rate may tell us that the baby will not be able to go through labor without being injured.

Some doctors and midwives question the use of monitors for everyone. They think monitoring can benefit some high-risk mothers. But it isn't of much value to mothers in the low-risk group. There are too many cesarean births, they say, because monitors are not always accurate. They would rather do careful **fetoscope** monitoring. A fetoscope is an instrument for listening to the internal sounds of the baby. It was used for years before electronic monitors.

But most doctors and midwives feel that without monitors it is much more difficult to tell if a baby is in trouble. They do further testing to be sure the reading is right. Then, if the baby's heart rate is still abnormal they will do a cesarean. It often saves the lives of the baby and the mother.

The nurse told Joyce she was running a temperature and losing a lot of water. The doctor wanted her to get into bed. She was put on an IV and hooked to an external fetal monitor.

Listening to the baby's heartbeat.

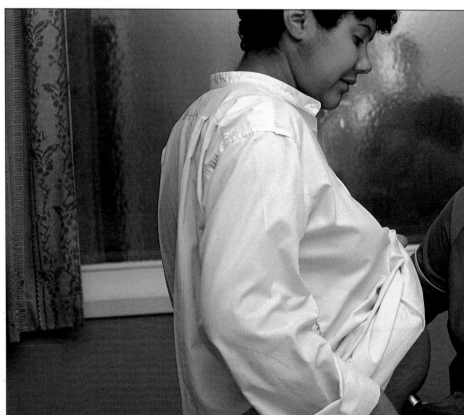

Active Phase

Toward the end of the early phase, the contractions will cause your cervix to dilate. You are now beginning the active phase. This phase may last from two to four hours. And your cervix will dilate from four to seven centimeters. The contractions will last longer and come closer together.

Whenever a contraction came, Joyce kept changing positions, trying to get comfortable. She had been talking a lot, but she stopped now.

Paul told her she was breathing too fast and taking in too much air. When the next contraction came Joyce began to breathe slower. With both hands, she rubbed her stomach in circles to help her relax. She'd learned that in her Lamaze class. Then, she concentrated on Flash, the stuffed dog she'd brought. And she took a deep breath before each contraction.

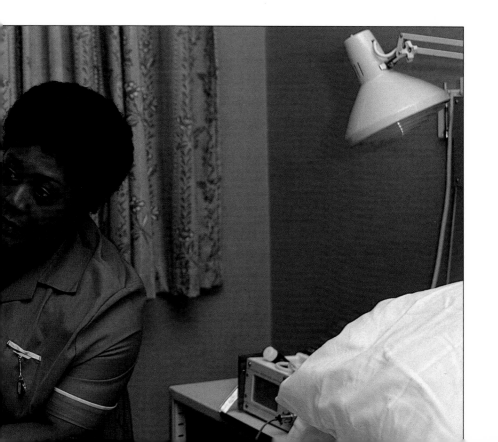

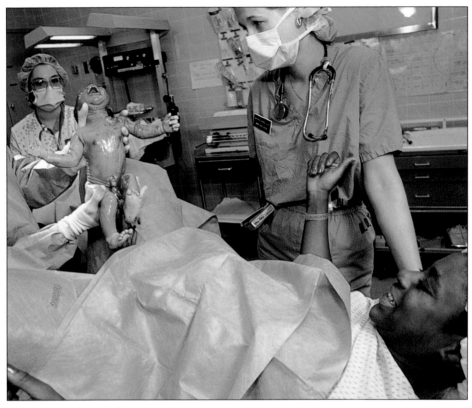

In the second stage of labor, the baby is delivered.

"You're doing great!" Paul said.

Women who haven't been prepared for childbirth often panic at this stage. Panic makes it impossible to relax. Some kind of pain-killer or anesthetic is often asked for and given.

Transition Stage

Transition is the shortest, and the most difficult, phase of the first stage of labor. It lasts from twenty to ninety minutes. Hard, strong contractions come every two or three minutes. They last sixty to ninety seconds. Sometimes they come one on top of the other.

Joyce felt the contractions over her entire stomach. Her back ached.

Paul massaged her back. Then he gave her a hot-water bottle and said again, "You're doing great!"

At this point, the cervix becomes fully dilated. It opens from seven to ten centimeters – the last part of the way. Delivery is almost here!

Because it's still too early, mothers should not give in to the urge to push as the baby continues down the birth canal. It's important to rest between contractions.

Joyce was perspiring heavily now. She felt weak and discouraged. She wanted to go home. Paul continued to hold her hand and tell her that she was doing great.

"I'm tired of hearing that," she said. "It's hot in here. I think I'm going to throw up."

Paul gave her some ice chips. "It's almost over now," he said. "Keep calm. It's not so bad, honey."

"Then why don't you have the baby?" she yelled.

The first stage of labor can take from one to more than twenty-four hours. For Joyce, it was about fourteen hours.

SECOND STAGE OF LABOR
Delivery

Ten centimeters! Your cervix is fully dilated, and contractions are coming every two to four minutes. They last from sixty to ninety seconds. You're feeling a strong urge to push now. It's the second stage of labor, time for the actual birth of your baby.

This stage may take from a few minutes to a couple of hours. It depends on how far down the baby is in the birth canal, and which part is coming down first. It also depends on how hard your uterus is contracting, and the force of your pushing.

Joyce's Cesarean

Paul, the nurse, and the doctor helped Joyce push. They tried to get three pushes out of each contraction. But after two more hours of labor, the baby still didn't come down. The doctor looked over the monitor readings of Joyce's contractions and the baby's heartbeat. She ordered some tests. When she got the results, she talked to Joyce and Paul about doing a **cesarean**. She said that if they waited any longer for a natural birth the baby might be damaged.

The young couple talked over their options with the doctor. They asked for another opinion. And when both doctors agreed, it was off to the delivery room for Joyce.

"I'm sorry," Joyce told Paul tearfully.

"No big deal," Paul said. "What matters is you, and a healthy baby. Man, I'm sure glad we're in this hospital."

The doctor told Joyce that she was going to cut from side to side just above the pubic bone. It was called a "bikini cut." When it healed, she said, the scar would hardly show.

An anesthetist came in and talked about the different anesthetics. The decision was made to give Joyce an **epidural** through a **catheter**, a thin, plastic tube. It would be given continuously in her back, and numb the lower part of her body. But the doctor carefully explained that the drugs wouldn't hurt the baby. And Joyce would be awake during the birth.

To Joyce, the epidural didn't feel any more painful than a regular shot. But about twenty minutes after it was given, she felt a tingling in her toes that kept spreading upward.

Then, the doctor inserted a catheter into her bladder to drain out the urine. She was told the tube would be removed the next day.

Next Joyce was scrubbed and covered with sterile sheets. And a low screen was placed across her chest. When all was ready, she asked for a mirror so she could see what was going on.

A nurse called Paul into the delivery room. Seated at the head of the operating table, he held Joyce's hand. As the doctor worked, Joyce felt pulling and pushing. But there was no pain.

After about five minutes the doctor put her hand under the head, and

The umbilical cord is cut.

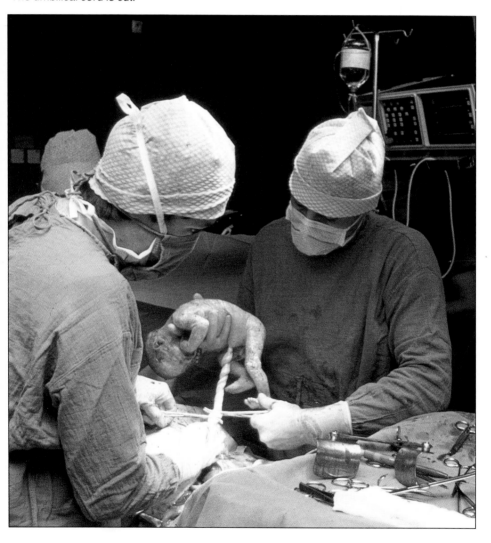

gently lifted the baby out. Fluid drained from its mouth and nose. Using a thin, plastic tube, the doctor carefully sucked out the fluid. The suctioning cleared the baby's throat so that it wouldn't inhale fluid into its lungs.

"It's a boy!" the doctor said, holding up the baby.

"His body was wet, bluish, and covered with something cheesy," Joyce said. "But his head was beautiful, and he was all cheeks."

Everyone smiled when Paul's camera clicked and he took baby Vance's first picture.

Gina's Experience in the ABC

When Gina reached the second stage of labor, she stayed right in her ABC birthing room. Because her cervix was no longer dilating, the next twenty contractions were much easier to deal with. This stage lasted for an hour. Then, she couldn't hold back any longer. The urge to push was overpowering.

Mothers used to deliver their babies in an upright position. They either stood, squatted, or sat on a birth stool. Later, the favored delivery position for mothers was lying on their backs in bed. Doctors then told women to give birth with their knees drawn up, in what is called the **lithotomy position**. Not long after, hospitals began using delivery tables with stirrups, instead of beds.

Now some mothers are going back to upright positions for birthing their babies. Their thinking is that when a mother lies on her back, the baby and the uterus press on a major vein.

While soft music played on the stereo, Gina pushed in a squatting position. She took a deep breath at the beginning of each contraction – and held it, exhaling hard. Until now, Gina's contractions helped mostly to dilate her cervix. The baby didn't move down much. But at this stage, the pressure she created helped to push the baby down the birth canal. As she pushed, her midwife kept track of the baby's heart rate with a fetoscope. Ed timed the contractions. Gina's mother rubbed her back. Having Ed and her mother there made Gina feel a whole lot better.

Gina's Episiotomy

If the doctor or midwife sees that the baby can't be born without tearing the mother, an **episiotomy** is done. An episiotomy is a cut of about an inch or so to make more room for the baby's head. Enlarging the vaginal opening keeps the muscles and ligaments from stretching. Stretching is thought to cause medical problems for the mother later on.

Another argument for an episiotomy is that a tiny cut is easier to sew than a large tear. Some doctors also think that an episiotomy is especially important when there's a big baby or a fast delivery. It also shortens the second stage of labor. And there is less time for the baby's head to push against the pelvic floor, which could cause brain damage.

Until recently, episiotomies were done on almost all mothers. Lately, though, since prepared childbirth has become popular in the United States, there have been fewer episiotomies. Most midwives in ABCs try not to do any cutting. They say it makes recovery longer and more uncomfortable. They also point out that normal tears are usually much smaller than an episiotomy. And they rarely go through muscle as episiotomies do.

If you aren't going to have an episiotomy, your doctor or midwife may massage the area with warm oil to stretch it. But it's important to listen carefully to the pushing instructions. Otherwise, you may tear after all.

When there is going to be an episiotomy, it is usually done between contractions. The cut is made just before the baby's head **crowns**. That means when it first shows at the opening of the vagina. Xylocaine, a local anesthetic similar to novocaine, is generally given to dull the pain. It doesn't affect the baby.

Gina hadn't planned on an episiotomy. But her baby was very large, and she had to have one. The midwife waited until the anesthesia had numbed the area. Then, with surgical scissors, she rapidly made the cut.

"The episiotomy didn't spoil our good birth experience," Gina said. "It's no fun to go through a long, hard delivery of a big baby and be ripped open. We decided it would be better if I had a small cut and got on with the delivery."

When the episiotomy was finished, Gina was told to push slowly again. Her vagina widened with each contraction. After about six contractions, the opening became a circle. Gina was ready to deliver.

Delivery means that the baby comes out of the birth canal into the world. It begins when the baby's head crowns and ends as the feet slip out. Looking down, Gina saw her baby's head. There was a lot of dark, wet hair plastered to its scalp.

At that moment, she felt a strong burning sensation and cried out. As with most babies, Gina's baby was coming out of the birth canal face down. The midwife told Gina to pant, but not to push.

Using both hands the midwife let the head come out slowly over one or two contractions. The cord was wrapped around the baby's neck, but that was no problem. She just slipped it over the head and shoulders. The shoulders were delivered one at a time as the baby's body rotated to one side.

Then the midwife gently suctioned the baby's mouth and nose. Once the shoulders were out, the chest slid out. It was quickly followed by the upper and lower arms.

A cry filled the birthing room, as Katti took her first breath. The midwife said, "It's a girl!"

For about a minute, the midwife held the baby's head down, a little below Gina's level. When the **umbilical cord** stopped throbbing, she attached two clamps, and made a cut between them. There are no nerve endings there so neither Gina nor the baby felt anything. The clamp closest to the body would be left on for twenty-four hours. Then the stub of the cord would dry and fall off.

After wiping Katti, the midwife put her on her side on Gina's chest. She stayed there for about fifteen minutes.

Joanne's Home Birth

The day Daniel was born Joanne awoke about five o'clock with strong contractions. "I was so excited," she said, "I couldn't stay in bed. So I got up and watched the birds at our feeder."

The contractions became more powerful. Joanne woke her mother and Craig. They put the sterilized sheets on her bed. Then she took a shower and began walking back and forth. Her bag of waters broke two hours later, and she was already in transition. Craig called the doctor and midwife and told them what was happening. When they came, Joanne got into bed. Sitting up and leaning against several pillows, she delivered, "With a lot of grunts," she said, laughingly. "And it seemed that the baby made the same grunts and groans that I did."

Joanne was pleased with her doctor. "Most doctors won't attend a home delivery," she said. "But my doctor was great. I was in control of the birth. And he was there to help if needed."

While the umbilical cord was still throbbing, Daniel was put on Joanne's chest. He began to nurse. Later, the midwife clamped the cord in two places. Craig used a scissors to cut the slick, tough cord between the clamps, and tied it off with a string.

You've birthed your baby and the cord has been cut. But you're not finished yet. The placenta, or afterbirth, must still be delivered. That's the third stage of labor.

THIRD STAGE OF LABOR

Delivery of the Placenta

The third stage of labor begins right after your baby is born. At this time, the placenta, a pancake-shaped organ that develops during pregnancy, separates from the wall of your uterus. Before birth, the placenta partly covered your unborn child. It was attached to the baby by the umbilical cord. After the baby's birth, it is sent into the vagina and delivered. This stage is also called afterbirth. It takes place quickly, usually in less than fifteen minutes.

When you feel contractions again don't think you're about to give birth to a twin. These contractions are helping the placenta separate by shrinking the size of your uterus. They will continue every few minutes until the placenta is delivered.

The placenta must come away completely from the uterus wall. Because the uterus is shedding, there is usually some bleeding. But if pieces are left in the uterus it could cause a hemorrhage (too much bleeding).

Soon after the baby is born, the placenta is delivered.

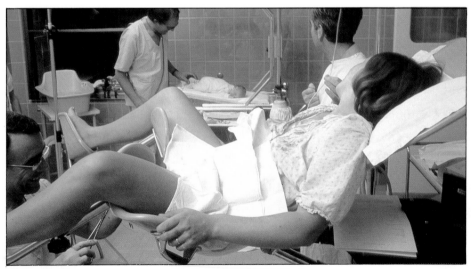

Joyce

After Vance's birth, **pitocin** was given in Joyce's IV line. Pitocin helps the uterus contract. Once the placenta was delivered, the doctor wiped out Joyce's abdomen. She inspected her uterus. Then she carefully lined up the layers of tissue and sewed the incisions.

Gina

After Katti was born, the midwife placed her hand lightly on Gina's stomach. She could feel the uterus shrinking as it changed from soft and flat to firm and round. She also knew that the placenta had already separated. That was because the uterus rose higher in Gina's abdomen. And the umbilical cord coming out of the vagina was longer.

Gina was told to push one last time. The midwife helped. She pressed down on Gina's stomach. And at the same time she pressed upward toward her navel. This kept the uterus tipped back. It also put pressure on it to send out the placenta. The midwife then pulled the umbilical cord gently downward as the placenta passed through the birth canal and into the vagina.

Gina said, "I felt a soft, warm sensation. It was nothing like the stretching and burning that I'd felt when the baby's head was delivered. Then there was a gush of blood and the placenta came out."

At this point, it's normal for the mother to lose one to two cups of blood. She can afford to lose it, because there has been a big increase in her blood supply during pregnancy.

Gina's midwife spread the placenta out in a basin and examined it carefully. She told Gina and Ed that it was normal and complete. The new parents asked to see it.

"It was dark red on the side that was attached, and shiny gray on the other side," Gina said. "And it had lots of blood vessels," Ed put in. The midwife told them it was about six inches across, and weighed a little over a pound. She took a blood sample from the end of the umbilical cord and sent it to the laboratory for tests. Then while Katti nursed, the midwife sewed Gina's episiotomy.

Joanne

The delivery of Joanne's placenta took place quickly. She thought it went fast because she had birthed Daniel in a sitting position. While the baby nursed, Joanne's uterus began to contract. The contractions came about two or three minutes apart.

In about ten minutes, without much help from the doctor, the placenta was delivered. The midwife then checked Joanne's uterus to see if it was firm and hard.

Most changes in the uterus happen in the first week or so after delivery. It takes about two months for it to return to its normal size and position.

Checking the Baby in the Hospital

Joyce's baby was weighed and measured. An ID bracelet with his mother's name was attached to his wrist. He was also footprinted. Joyce got a copy of the footprints for Vance's baby book. Then the baby was bathed, wrapped in a towel, and placed under a radiant warmer where the pediatrician checked him. Babies are born wet in cool delivery rooms and lose body heat quickly. They must be kept covered so they won't get cold.

The umbilical cord will be clamped closer to the infant's skin so that only a short stump remains. And usually erythomycin ointment will be applied to the baby's eyes. In most cases, some type of eye medication is required by law. It protects newborns against bacteria which cause blindness.

Some hospitals give other medicines too, including a vitamin K shot. It helps the newborn's blood to clot.

48

The Apgar Storing System

The nurse, doctor, or midwife will probably examine your baby at one, five, and ten minutes after birth. Then, the infant's health will be rated on a scale of one to ten according to the **Apgar Scoring System**. The scoring system was named for Dr. Virginia Apgar, who developed it.

A total score of seven or above means the baby has adjusted well to the outside world. Lower than seven tells us that the infant may have a problem.

There are those who think that this system of scoring a newborn's health isn't very reliable. They say it rates too few things. And they object because all scoring is done in the first ten minutes of life, instead of over a longer period. Finally, it is only one person's opinion of how the baby's health rates.

APGAR SCORING SYSTEM			
Points	0	1	2
Heart Rate (Pulse)	not detectable	below 100	above 100
Respiratory Effort (Breathing)	absent	slow, irregular	strong, good crying
Muscle Tone	limp	some flexion or arms and legs	active, good motion
Reflex Irritability	no response	grimace	cough, sneeze, or cry
Color **White Child**	blue, pale	body pink; extremities blue	completely pink
Black Child	grayish, pale	body strong color; extremities grayish	strong color; lips pink; palms, soles of feet pink

FOURTH STAGE OF LABOR

Recovery

Recovery, the fourth stage of labor, takes place an hour or two after the placenta is delivered. Your baby's health was checked in the delivery room. Now it's your turn to be checked. It's important at this time to keep your bleeding under control.

Hospital-birth Recovery

In the hospital, there is a special room set aside for recovery. Your stay there is from two to six hours. A nurse will check your temperature at the beginning and end of this time. You may be up and around immediately. Or you could be kept in bed for a while. It depends on where you deliver, and what type of anesthetic was used.

Sometimes your support person is permitted to stay in the recovery room with you. If you have arranged beforehand with your doctor or pediatrician, your baby may stay there too. If not, the baby will be taken to the nursery.

After Joyce's cesarean, the nurse cleaned up the baby and handed him to Paul. When Joyce was wheeled to the recovery room, Vance came too – in his father's arms. The new family were together there for about two hours.

In the recovery room your blood pressure, breathing, and pulse will be checked about every fifteen minutes. You'll probably be thirsty. Drink lots of liquids. They will replace the fluids that you lost during labor and delivery.

After the Hospital Recovery Room

At this point, most new mothers are taken to a room on the obstetrical floor. The average hospital stay after a normal vaginal delivery is two to three

After delivery, the baby is cleaned and covered.

days, for a cesarean four to five days. During this time, your episiotomy, uterus, and breasts will be checked by the doctor, midwife, or nurse.

Almost all new mothers have some tenderness in the **perineum**. For a few days, whether you've had stitches or not, it will feel sore. An ice pack helps relieve pain. Later, you can take warm-water baths (sitz baths).

Keep clean and comfortable. Try to do things for yourself instead of being waited on. You'll get stronger much faster.

The Uterus

Your uterus, which had been enlarged for so long, is now a small, hard ball. At the top (fundus) there are open blood vessels where the placenta has separated. As the uterus contracts, it clamps off these vessels. This prevents too much bleeding while the uterus is going back to its normal size and shape.

Bladder and Bowels

Walk to the bathroom as soon as possible. But ask for help at first. Try to urinate about every few hours for the first day or so. The perineum has been stretched and pushed on for quite some time during labor. You may not have much feeling there. But if you do the **kegels** (pelvic floor exercises) you learned in your childbirth classes, feeling will return. Kegels will also strengthen your muscles and help you heal faster.

A full bladder at this time can be painful, because it pushes up against the uterus. It can also cause more bleeding and make your blood pressure rise. If you can't urinate after a few hours, a catheter may be placed in your bladder. When the bladder empties, the sterile tube is removed. It's better not to have to use a catheter, though, because you may be sore. And it could lead to a bladder infection.

Some hospitals won't let you go home until you've had a bowel movement. You may think a BM will be painful and pop your stitches open. But your stitches won't break, and there is usually little or no pain. Sometimes a mild enema or laxative is given to new mothers. Prune juice may help too.

Lochia

Lochia is the vaginal discharge that begins after delivery of the placenta. It is a mixture of blood and uterus lining. For about three days the lochia is bright red. After that, there will be less lochia, and the color will fade. The discharge lasts for about six weeks. You'll be given a sanitary belt and pad. Don't use tampons until your doctor or midwife says it's okay.

Breast Changes

Breast milk usually comes in about the third day. If you're planning to bottle-feed, the doctor will give you medication to dry your milk. Even with medicine to prevent it, you may have some milk. But don't nurse your baby. Nursing will make you produce more milk. If your breasts are full and painful, wear a tight bra or breast binder for relief.

If you are going to nurse your baby, keep your nipples clean. Use breast cream on them after each feeding to prevent cracking and drying. Your breasts will become quite full now. Wear a nursing bra for support.

Cramps, or Afterbirth Pains

Afterbirth pains similar to menstrual cramps begin right after the placenta is delivered. They continue for a few days. But they aren't too bad with the first baby. The reason for the pains is that your uterus is getting back into shape. And it's beginning to go down into its normal position. For relief from pain, massage your uterus, especially before nursing. Relaxation and breathing exercises can also help get you through these few days.

Don't take pain medicine unless you really need it. If you must have it, the doctor or midwife will give you a mild pain-killer. Take the medicine about a half-hour before feedings, if you are nursing.

Rooming-In

Many hospitals let newborns room-in with their mothers. The thinking is that infants will be more content than if they spend all their time in a nursery. Some mothers choose to have their babies room-in during the day and sleep in the nursery at night. Others prefer to have the baby stay in the nursery and be brought in only for feedings. Whether your infant rooms-in full or part-time, use the time you are together to get acquainted. Hold and cuddle the little one.

Recovery at the Birth Center

After Katti's birth, Gina was kept in the same room during recovery. Ed and her mother stayed there too. The baby went to the nursery for weighing and checking, and then roomed-in with Gina.

After her episiotomy was stitched, Gina had an ice pack for her bottom to help with the soreness and swelling. The midwife kept a close check on Gina's uterus and vital signs.

Gina felt a little dizzy. So her mother helped her walk to the shower room. Afterwards, the nurse made them a snack in the birth center kitchen. It was late, and they were tired, so Gina and Ed decided to sleep overnight at the birth center. The baby slept beside them in a small bed.

Gina's mother went home to get things ready. And the new family joined her at home early the next morning.

Recovery After Home Birth

The midwife stayed for about two hours after Joanne birthed Daniel. She checked Joanne's uterus often, to make sure that the bleeding was under control. Joanne needed a few stitches and the midwife took care of it. If the tear was larger, Joanne would have had to go to a hospital. The midwife gave her the baby to nurse. She told Joanne it was especially important to nurse when the baby is delivered at home. Nursing helps the uterus contract and control bleeding.

After nursing, Joanne's mother helped her get to the bathroom. Joanne took a shower and washed her hair. The new family toasted Daniel's birth with a pitcher of orange juice. Then Joanne took a nap.

Before You Go Home From the Hospital or ABC

Don't be afraid to ask your doctor, midwife, or pediatrician questions. If possible, attend a baby-care class. Learn to diaper, bathe, and dress your child. Get feeding instructions from nurses in the nursery.

Some hospitals and birthing centers give a celebration dinner for the new mother and a guest of her choice.

Joyce said, "Paul and I felt very special at our celebration dinner. We had steak and champagne. And our baby was there too." If your hospital or birthing center doesn't do it, plan your own celebration.

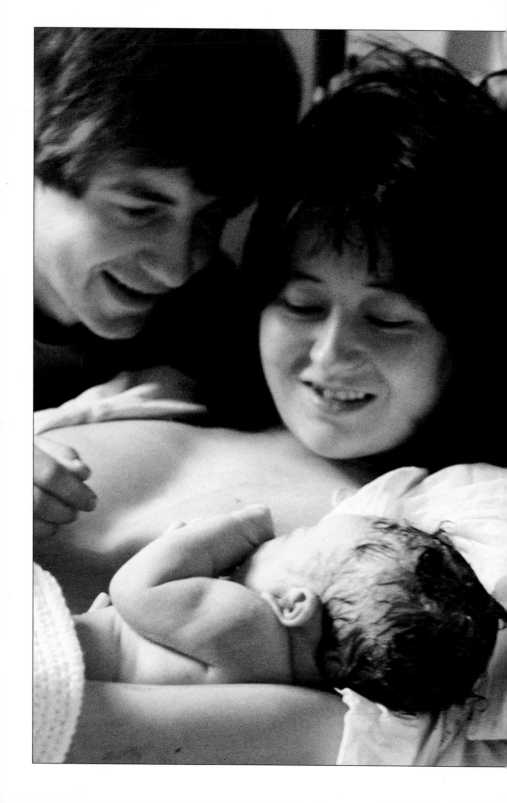

Chapter Six:
After Your Child is Born

The arrival of your baby is a big event, but it is also a big responsibility. Having spent so many months getting ready for your baby's birth, it's only natural if you feel tired and a little let down at first.

Postpartum Blues

Now you've had a baby there are many changes in your life.The main one is that you are in charge of a live human being. You've planned and waited for this to happen. You should be happy. So why do you feel like crying most of the time?

You have what's called **postpartum** (afterbirth) **blues**. It happens to many new mothers, especially those with first babies. About the third day after delivery, body changes, tiredness, pain, and sometimes disappointment bring it on.

Talk to your nurse. She's familiar with the blues and can tell you how to cope with them. Usually they only last a few days.

Fathers, too, face changes. They can become loving partners sharing in the care of the infant. Or they can feel left out and unwanted. Share your feelings with your partner. You are now a family.

Bonding

Joyce didn't want to be separated from her baby right after birth. She asked for time to bond with him as soon as possible.

"When we were in the recovery room with Vance," Paul said, "we held him, and talked softly to him. He looked around a lot, and seemed to listen for the sound of our voices."

Gina and Ed had a good bonding experience too. Gina kept Katti close to her while she nursed. When she finished, Ed picked Katti up and held her against his skin.

"Her eyes were wide open," Ed said. "They seemed to smile right into mine."

Joanne and Craig found bonding easy at home. "I nursed the baby and held him for a long time," Joanne said. "Then Grandma bathed him, and we celebrated with an orange juice toast. Each of us took turns holding and patting Daniel."

If You Can't Bond Immediately

If your baby has a medical problem and is kept in a nursery, you can bond later. The baby's health comes first. Ask your coach to go there. The first bonding can take place between them. If your baby has to stay in the nursery, visit often. Try your best to get to know your child.

Circumcision

Parents of a baby boy have to decide whether or not to circumcise their son. **Circumcision** is an operation where the foreskin of the penis is cut off. The foreskin is a double layer of skin. It covers the tip of the penis.

Circumcision is one of the oldest operations we know of. It is practiced by many religions. The main non-religious reason for circumcision is cleanliness. It was once thought to prevent diseases and infections.

Lately, however, there has been some new thinking about circumcision. Many doctors say that the surgery is not necessary. They point out that good personal cleanliness habits can have the same results as circumcision. Whether or not your son will be circumcised is up to you and his father. Think about the pros and cons and make your decision.

There is very little pain from the surgery. And although there have been some cases of infection, bleeding, and injury, there usually isn't anything to worry about.

Advice to the New Mother
When you are home, enjoy your baby. But don't become a hermit. Talk to your partner. Keep in touch with your family and friends.

During the first days and weeks you'll probably feel tired. Be sure to get enough rest. Take naps when the baby sleeps.

Try to look your very best. Take showers, do your hair, and wear makeup. Dress up every so often. Go out for walks. Do the exercises your doctor or midwife gave you to get back in shape.

A Safe Delivery and a Healthy Baby!
We hope this book has helped to take some of the mystery out of childbirth. When you know what is going to happen you will be able to handle labor and delivery without fear.

No matter how you deliver your baby, vaginally or by cesarean, childbirth takes a great deal of courage on your part. Your baby's birth is something very special. You should be proud to be a mother.

Here's to a safe labor, a joyous delivery, and a healthy mother and baby!

Glossary

Alternative birthing center (ABC) – labor, delivery, and recovery take place in one room.

Amnion – the thin, tough, innermost membrane enclosing the unborn baby.

Amniotic fluid – the liquid in which the unborn baby floats throughout pregnancy. It keeps the baby comfortable.

Anesthetic – a substance given to take away feeling in a part of the body.

Apgar Scoring System – a system for scoring the well-being of newborns after examinations at one, three, and five minutes after birth.

Bag of waters – sac with amniotic fluid which surrounds the baby.

Birth educator – person who teaches a childbirth class.

Birthing room – a room in a hospital where labor, delivery, and recovery takes place.

Bloody show – thick mucous plug hidden in the vagina during pregnancy. When the mucous plug comes out, labor is near.

Bonding – a special feeling of closeness and love between newborns and parents that continues throughout life.

Catheter – a long, thin, hollow tube through which fluids can drain out of a place such as the bladder, or be put into a place such as the spine.

Certified nurse-midwife – a registered nurse who has worked with pregnant women for at least a year. After finishing a graduate midwifery program at school, the nurse must pass a written exam to get a license.

Cervix – the lower part of the uterus. It thins and opens to allow for the baby's birth.

Cesarean delivery – birth of a bab through cuts (incisions) in the abdome and uterus.

Chorion – the outer membrane enclosin the unborn baby.

Circumcision – a procedure that involve removal of the foreskin from the penis.

Crowns – the baby's head first shows a the opening of the vagina during delivery

Dilate – the steady opening (widening) of the cervix, which helps to get the birt canal ready for delivery.

Efface – the thinning (shortening) of th cervix, which helps to get the birth cana ready for delivery.

Epidural – a local anesthetic give through a catheter.

Episiotomy – the cutting of the perine tissues during delivery to make a large opening for the delivery of the baby head.

Fetal monitor – a machine used to recor the mother's contractions and the baby heartbeat on a graph, as well as on digital readout (computer). If the baby is i trouble, an internal monitor, which consist of a scalp probe and/or a uterine cathete may be used to get more information abou the baby.

Fetoscope – an instrument like a steth scope, used to listen to fetal heartbea and see how the baby is responding stress of labor contractions.

Fetus – term by which the unborn baby called after the first trimester of pregnanc until delivery of the head.

High-risk unit – highly technical equip ment and personnel for mothers an babies who can have complicated prob lems with delivery.

egel – an exercise referring to the squeezing in and up of the vagina to tighten and strengthen the pelvic floor.

abia – folds of tissue of the female external sex organs.

abor – the muscular contractions of the uterus that push the baby downward into the birth canal and out into the world.

abor coach – usually is the baby's father, but may be any person who helps and gives support to the mother-to-be.

ithotomy position – giving birth lying in bed with knees drawn up.

ochia – the vaginal discharge that begins after delivery of the placenta.

Midwife – can be a certified nurse-midwife (CNM) or a lay midwife.

Mucous plug – also called the "bloody show." Thick mucus hidden in vagina during pregnancy.

Obstetrical (OB) – relates to the medical profession of obstetrics or the care of women during and after pregnancy.

Pediatrician – a doctor who treats infants and children and treats their diseases.

Pelvis – the hip bone housing the pelvic organs.

Perineum – the area of a woman's body from the urethra and vagina to the rectum.

Pitocin – a drug that changes slow-moving labor to a more normal pace.

Placenta – a pancake-shaped organ developed during pregnancy to which one end of the umbilical cord is attached.

Postpartum blues – body changes, tiredness, pain and sometimes disappointment bring on unhappy feelings about the third day after delivery.

Prepared childbirth – natural childbirth – natural delivery.

Prepping – pubic shave and enema.

Presentation – the part of the baby's body that presents, or shows, itself first at delivery – usually the head.

Station – where the baby's head is in relation to the ischial spines (the three major bones that make up the pelvis).

Trimester – a period of three months. Pregnancy is divided into three trimesters.

Umbilical cord – a flexible type of cord connecting the fetus at the navel with the placenta. It has two arteries and a vein that feed the fetus and take away its wastes.

Uterus – a hollow, muscular organ in women, located in the pelvis behind the bladder.

Vagina – a passageway from the outside of a woman's body to the uterus.

ACKNOWLEDGEMENTS

The author and editor wish to express their appreciation to the following who have been of great assistance in the preparation of this book:

Dr. David Turow, Board Certified specialist in Obstetrics and Gynecology, Rush North Shore Medical Center, Skokie, Illinois; Deborah Zage, Clinical Nurse Specialist, Deborah Desmarais, Patient Care Manager in Obstetrics/Labor and Delivery, Eileen Zurick, Assistant Patient Care Manager in Obstetrics/Labor and Delivery, Highland Park Hospital, Highland Park, Illinois; Joanne Simcoe, Registered Nurse, Mt. Sinai Hospital, Chicago; and Carolee Zupsich, Certified Nurse Midwife.

With special thanks to Joyce and Paul Somerstorfer, Gina and Ed Jablenski, and Joanne and Craig Simcoe, and their families.

Index

Photographic Credits
page 4: Zefa; page 6: Robert Harding; page 8: Hutchison Library; pages 16, 32 and 36-37: Sally and Richard Greenhill; page 22: Science Photo Library; pages 30 and 56: Network/Barry Lewis; page 38: Anthea Sieveking/Vision International; pages 41 and 46: Rex Features; page 50: Magnum.